AI WORLD
AI AT WORK

by Ford Chambers

pogo

Ideas for Parents and Teachers

Pogo Books let children practice reading informational text while introducing them to nonfiction features such as headings, labels, sidebars, maps, and diagrams, as well as a table of contents, glossary, and index.

Carefully leveled text with a strong photo match offers early fluent readers the support they need to succeed.

Before Reading

- "Walk" through the book and point out the various nonfiction features. Ask the student what purpose each feature serves.
- Look at the glossary together. Read and discuss the words.

Read the Book

- Have the child read the book independently.
- Invite them to list questions that arise from reading.

After Reading

- Discuss the child's questions. Talk about how they might find answers to those questions.
- Prompt the child to think more. Ask: Would you like a job working with AI? Why or why not?

Pogo Books are published by Jump!
5357 Penn Avenue South
Minneapolis, MN 55419
www.jumplibrary.com

Copyright © 2025 Jump!
International copyright reserved in all countries. No part of this book may be reproduced in any form without written permission from the publisher.

Library of Congress Cataloging-in-Publication Data

Names: Chambers, Ford, author.
Title: AI at work / by Ford Chambers.
Description: Minneapolis, MN: Jump!, Inc., [2025]
Series: AI world | Includes index.
Audience: Ages 7–10
Identifiers: LCCN 2024034695 (print)
LCCN 2024034696 (ebook)
ISBN 9798892135566 (hardcover)
ISBN 9798892135573 (paperback)
ISBN 9798892135580 (ebook)
Subjects: LCSH: Artificial intelligence—Industrial applications—Juvenile literature. | Artificial intelligence—Juvenile literature.
Classification: LCC TA347.A78 C435 2025 (print)
LCC TA347.A78 (ebook)
DDC 006.3—dc23/eng/20240823
LC record available at https://lccn.loc.gov/2024034695
LC ebook record available at https://lccn.loc.gov/2024034696

Editor: Alyssa Sorenson
Designer: Emma Almgren-Bersie

Photo Credits: IM Imagery/Shutterstock, cover; kung_tom/Shutterstock, 1; natatravel/iStock, 3; Ira Lichi/Shutterstock, 4; Suwin66/Shutterstock, 5; Laurence Dutton/iStock, 6-7; Hugh Mitton/Alamy, 8; Amorn Suriyan/iStock, 9; miodrag ignjatovic/iStock, 10-11; Alexey_Rezvykh/Shutterstock, 12-13; efired/iStock, 14-15; VioletaStoimenova/iStock, 16-17; Prostock-studio/Shutterstock, 18 (hands); panuwat phimpha/Shutterstock, 18 (screen); Gorodenkoff/Shutterstock, 19; VesnaArt/Shutterstock, 20-21; katleho Seisa/iStock, 21; PhonlamaiPhoto/iStock, 23.

Printed in the United States of America at Corporate Graphics in North Mankato, Minnesota.

TABLE OF CONTENTS

CHAPTER 1
What Is AI? 4

CHAPTER 2
AI on the Job 8

CHAPTER 3
Future AI Jobs 18

ACTIVITIES & TOOLS
Try This! 22
Glossary 23
Index 24
To Learn More 24

CHAPTER 1
WHAT IS AI?

You are at a restaurant. Instead of a person, a **robot** greets you! It brings you to your table. It even brings your food.

robot server

How does the robot know what to do? It uses **artificial intelligence** (AI)! Robots are controlled by computers. AI lets computers do things humans use knowledge and skills to do. AI even understands language. It can make jobs easier.

AI **chatbots** are one example. People ask chatbots to do tasks. Like what? A teacher can ask a chatbot to make quiz questions. Now, the teacher doesn't have to. They can spend more time helping their students!

AI helps companies, too. How? If workers use AI, they may be able to get more things done. They do it faster. This makes the company more money.

CHAPTER 1

CHAPTER 2
AI ON THE JOB

AI does many jobs. Driving is one. Some taxis have AI. They drive by themselves. They pick people up. They follow the rules of the road. They get people where they need to go safely.

AI helps doctors, too. It can look at **MRI** images. AI tells the doctor what it sees. It can find **cancer**.

CHAPTER 2

AI works with **customers**. How? Tia ordered something online. It is being mailed to her. But she has not gotten it yet. She asks the company where it is. AI tracks the package. It answers. This helps human workers at the company. How? They are free to answer harder customer questions. The company can help more people.

DID YOU KNOW?

Some types of customer service AI do the work of 250 people!

CHAPTER 2 | 11

AI helps **manufacture**, too. Companies that make cars use AI robots! These robots do a lot of tasks. Some **weld**. Others polish car parts.

DID YOU KNOW?

Manufacturers use AI to design products. AI makes **blueprints**. Workers follow the instructions.

12 CHAPTER 2

CHAPTER 2

AI robots can clean! They use **sensors** to know what is around them. This helps human cleaners. They have time for other tasks.

AI can help companies sell their products. How? AI writes text. **Marketers** put this text in emails. They send it to many people. They use the text in **social media** posts, too. AI can save workers a lot of time! But workers still need to check what AI writes. Why? AI is not always correct. The text may be wrong. People may need to fix things.

TAKE A LOOK!

What jobs use AI the most? Take a look!

INFORMATION-RELATED JOBS

EDUCATION

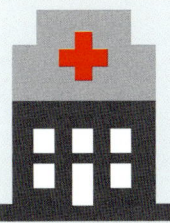

HEALTH CARE

MANUFACTURING

FINANCE

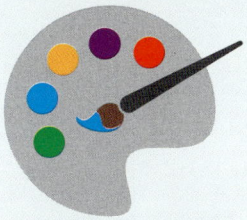

ARTS AND ENTERTAINMENT

REAL ESTATE

MANAGEMENT

TECH SERVICE

CHAPTER 3
FUTURE AI JOBS

Companies will keep using AI in the future. AI will get smarter. It will do more. Customers will get better service. Workers will get more help.

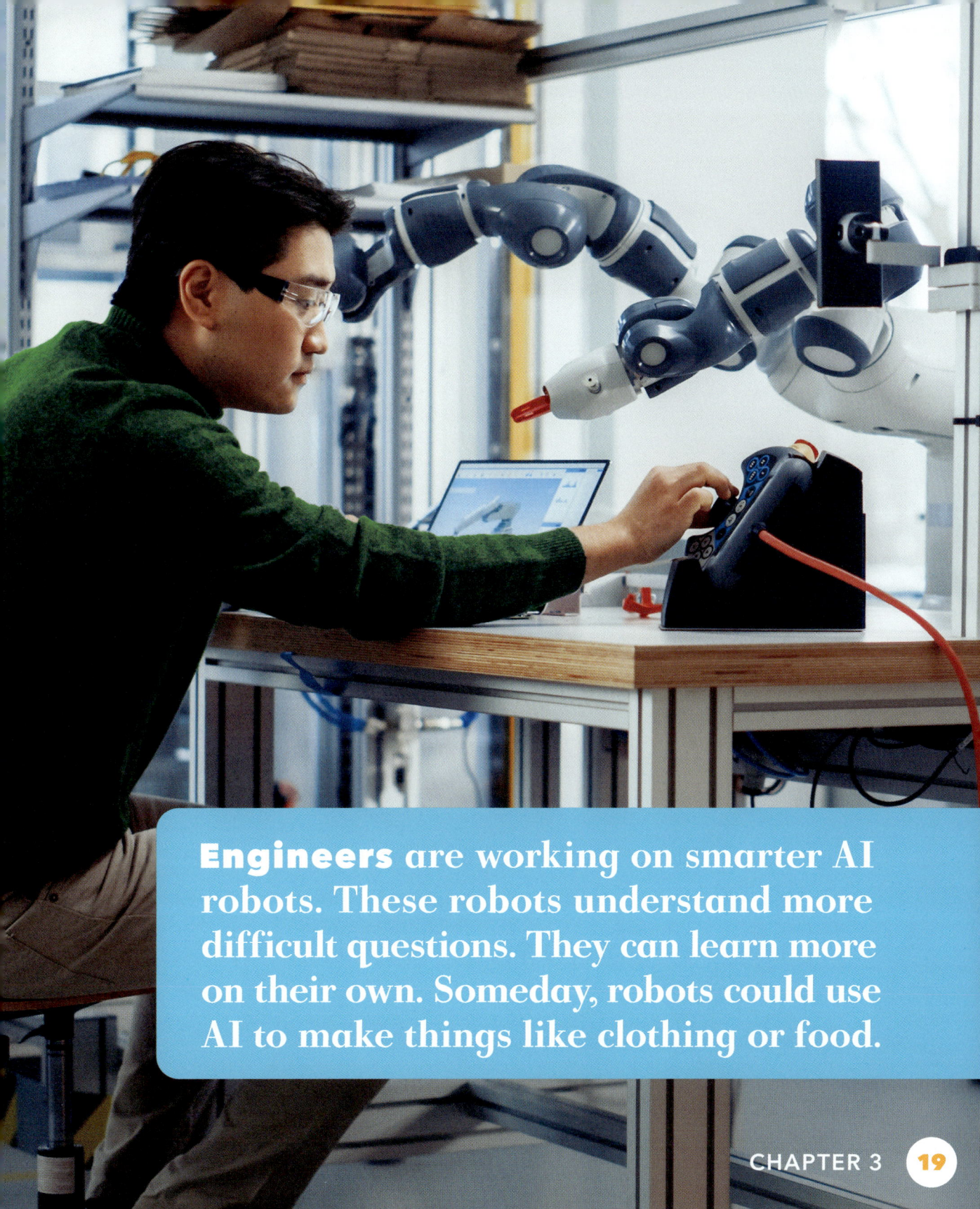

Engineers are working on smarter AI robots. These robots understand more difficult questions. They can learn more on their own. Someday, robots could use AI to make things like clothing or food.

CHAPTER 3 19

CHAPTER 3

AI could replace humans for some jobs. But AI also creates jobs. Companies will need more people who can work with AI. Would you like to work with AI?

DID YOU KNOW?

In 2024, 5.4 percent of U.S. companies used AI. That number will likely grow.

ACTIVITIES & TOOLS

TRY THIS!

GIVE AI A JOB

What work could AI do? Come up with some new AI jobs with this fun activity!

What You Need:
- paper and pencil or a device for taking notes

① Come up with an idea for a company. What does it do? Does it sell products? Does it provide services for customers? Write down your ideas.

② Think about how your company works. How do customers find you? Do you have a store? Do you have a website? Write down your thoughts.

③ What sort of things do your workers do? List everything you can think of.

④ Which of these tasks could AI do? Could AI do jobs at your company that human workers can't? Write down your ideas! Share them with a friend or family member.

GLOSSARY

artificial intelligence: The science of making computers do things that previously needed human intelligence, such as understanding language.

blueprints: Detailed design plans that show how something should be built.

cancer: A serious disease in which some cells in the body grow faster than normal cells and destroy healthy organs and tissues.

chatbots: Computer programs that communicate with people.

customers: People who buy goods or services from a company.

engineers: People who create, build, and work on machines.

manufacture: To make something on a large scale using special equipment or machinery.

marketers: People who advertise or promote something so people want to buy it.

MRI: A procedure that takes computerized images of the inside of a person's body.

robot: A machine that is programmed to perform complex human tasks.

sensors: Tools that notice and measure changes for a device.

social media: Websites and applications that let users create online communities in which they share messages, images, and other content.

weld: To join two pieces of metal by heating them until they melt together.

ACTIVITIES & TOOLS 23

INDEX

blueprints 12
cars 12
chatbots 6
clean 14
companies 6, 11, 12, 16, 18, 21
computers 5
customers 11, 18
design 12
driving 8
engineers 19
language 5
manufacture 12, 17
marketers 16
questions 6, 11, 19
restaurant 4
robot 4, 5, 12, 14, 19
sensors 14
social media 16
taxis 8
tracks 11
weld 12
writes 16

TO LEARN MORE

Finding more information is as easy as 1, 2, 3.
1. Go to www.factsurfer.com
2. Enter "AIatwork" into the search box.
3. Choose your book to see a list of websites.